Prince William

Prince William

Alison Gauntlett

Photographs by the
Daily Mail

p

For Charles and Brenda

This is a Parragon Book
First published in 2003

Parragon
Queen Street House
4 Queen Street
Bath, BA1 IHE, UK

All photographs © Associated Newspapers Archive
Text © Parragon

Produced by Atlantic Publishing Ltd
Origination by Croxons PrePress
Designed by John Dunne

A catalogue record for this book is available from the British Library.

ISBN 1 40540 312 8

Printed in China

Introduction

Twenty-one on the 21st June 2003, Prince William is second in line to the throne. From the moment he drew his first breath, the world has watched the life of this remarkable young man. His parents, the Prince and Princess of Wales, were determined that he would lead as normal a life as possible and were committed to providing him with as much love and attention as they could give. The birth of his brother Harry, just over two years later, completed the family.

The formality and tradition of the Royal Family were, at times, questioned by his mother, Diana, which led to a much more informal upbringing. He mixed with other children from a much earlier age than previous royal children, attended schools specifically selected by his parents and has been allowed to make many more decisions for himself.

At six feet two, he is the image of his mother and has inherited many of her mannerisms and her gift for communicating with people. He has also inherited his father's love of the countryside and outdoor pursuits, and his talent for painting and shooting. An outstanding athlete, William is happiest in an environment when he is totally anonymous and can contribute at the same level as everyone else, without any special privileges. He made full use of his gap year when he was able to travel and make a difference to other people's lives, often living in very challenging conditions and thriving on these experiences.

His life was turned upside down by his mother's tragic death when he was only fifteen. He adored Diana and she in turn was totally devoted to her two boys. She was often very dependent on William, as her marriage to Prince Charles gradually broke down. After the funeral, the stability of Eton, and strong family relationships, helped William and his brother face up to the life ahead of them. He has grown even closer to Harry and his father, as he has matured into a charming and good-looking young man, renowned for knowing his own mind. His mother has left him a wonderful legacy.

Packed with more than 150 photographs from the archives of the *Daily Mail*, many of which have never been published, this book captures the first 21 years in the life of a remarkable young man who will, one day, become King.

Prince William

William, second in line to the throne, was born on 21 June 1982. The whole country waited to hear news of the first-born child to the Prince and Princess of Wales. His parents broke with Royal tradition and William Arthur Philip Louis was born at St Mary's in Paddington, not Buckingham Palace. As soon as Prince Charles and Princess Diana carried him out of the hospital 36 hours later, the eyes of the world were upon him and have remained so ever since.

Charles and Diana were determined that he would lead as normal a life as possible. Although Barbara Barnes was employed as his first nanny, both parents spent as much time with him as they could, often taking over meal times and bath times and Diana was always the one who would look after him at night if he was ill. In the spring of 1983, a tour of Australia was planned and William travelled with them – Charles was determined that his children would not endure the long separations from their parents that he had experienced.

Brother Harry was born in September 1984. Despite Diana's concerns of potential sibling rivalry, William was captivated by his baby brother. The two boys have always been very close, with William playing the older brother role and very much the protector of Harry.

This bond, early established, would help both of them in the years to come.

It was decided that William would attend a kindergarten rather than be educated at home in his early years. This would enable him to forge his own friendships and enjoy pre-school education in a more disciplined environment. After four terms in Miss Mynors' kindergarten he then spent his pre-prep years at Wetherby in Notting Hill. It was here that he showed the first signs of the excellence in sport that he would later on enjoy. Mixing with other children was sometimes a challenge. He was quick-witted and soon learned to pull rank in playground arguments – at times his personal bodyguard would need to intervene. However, with maturity and the discipline of school life, this soon disappeared.

During his years at Wetherby, his parents' marriage was rapidly disintegrating and Charles had moved to Highgrove. William and his brother Harry only saw their father at weekends. In September 1990 William began his prep years at Ludgrove in Berkshire. Both parents had agreed that he would attend a boarding school where it was hoped that the discipline would help him settle down and understand his future role in life.

In December 1992, Diana visited the school to tell William that she and Prince Charles would be officially

separating – it was to be announced in the House of Commons the next day. 'I hope you will both be happier now' was his response. In many ways it helped that he was at boarding school – he was protected from the press and had not had to witness his parents' arguments. Diana had a very close relationship with William and frequently referred to him as 'the man in my life'. She would often take him into her confidence and he in turn would try to cheer her up when she was down.

Prince Charles employed Tiggy Legge-Bourke the following year to act as friend and mentor to the boys whenever they were staying with him. She loved the outdoors and any kind of sport and William quickly forged an excellent relationship with her. Her great sense of humour and fun ensured that she could reach the boys at their level, but at the same time play a part when they needed advice and reassurance.

William passed the Common Entrance examination and began his school career at Eton College in September 1995. He settled into the school's life easily and successfully. By now he was much happier to be anonymous and the ethos at Eton meant he could be treated equally and always be well cared for. He achieved academic and sporting success. By the time he left he had passed 9 GCSEs and 3 'A' levels, had been selected for his year's First XI in football and had broken swimming records. He also rowed, played rugby and water polo and continued to ride horses.

His life was shattered when his father woke him on 31 August 1997 to tell him that his mother was dead.

From that moment he had to endure the intrusion of the press, the formality of the Royal Family and the very public nature of the funeral as well as coping with his own emotions. He became even more protective of Harry and from that day his relationship with Charles strengthened. He blamed the paparazzi for her death and this fuelled his reticence in the face of reporters and photographers in the years to come.

William and Harry coped amazingly well with the trauma of the funeral. They followed the cortège for a mile as it made its way to Westminster Abbey. He was later to admit that most of the day had been a complete blur. They returned to Highgrove with their father and Tiggy joined them as they gave the boys every encouragement to talk about their mother and the events that surrounded her death. William was keen to return to Eton where he could be back in its protective atmosphere, away from the press and with people and friends he could trust.

William was maturing fast and it was becoming apparent that he would grow into a very good-looking young man. He had an incredible likeness to his mother, with the same engaging smile. It was during a visit to

Canada in 1998 that his confidence and maturity began to emerge. His winning smile attracted groups of screaming teenage girls and he began to feel more at ease in the public limelight and happier about meeting the public on walkabouts.

In his final year at Eton he decided that he would go to university and gained a place at St Andrews to read History of Art. However, he was determined to make good use of his planned gap year. His aim was to get as far away as possible from his life as a Royal. He wanted to go to other parts of the world where he wouldn't be recognised and where he would be treated as an equal with no special favours. He eventually chose to spend time in Chile with Raleigh International; to go on safari in southern Africa; work as labourer on a farm in south-west England; and travel to Belize with the Welsh Guards on a jungle exercise. At times he lived in very basic conditions, enduring hardship and very challenging situations. It was obvious afterwards that he had thrived on these experiences and derived a great deal of pleasure from helping other people. Those that had worked with him were hugely impressed by his leadership skills, teamwork and determination.

At St Andrews University, William is intent on keeping a low profile while he completes his studies. It is likely that once he finishes his degree he will spend some time in the armed forces. However, he also now needs to learn about Britain and how every system of government works in preparation for his future role as King. He will be expected to find out first hand by visiting offices, observing meetings and meeting key personnel. He will need to learn how to make speeches and will be expected to accompany his father on official occasions.

William is a young man who is determined to live life to the full. He has a great sense of fun, is a very talented athlete and has a good academic background. He has had to endure much more trauma during his life than many others of his age, but he has emerged as a charming and confident young man who knows his own mind. He has been left a great legacy by his mother and will no doubt honour her continual advice – 'Be your own man'.

Prince William

Welcome Prince William

William was born at 9.03pm on June 21st 1982, at St Mary's Hospital in Paddington, London. He weighed in at 7lb 1oz and was born after a 16-hour induced labour. It had been a very public pregnancy with much written in the press. Following the wishes of his parents he was born in hospital rather than in Buckingham Palace.

Opposite and left: His proud parents emerged from the hospital the following day and after a brief photo call were driven to Kensington Palace. It was another seven days before his name was officially announced as William Arthur Philip Louis.

Below: Many of the cheering well-wishers who greeted them had waited for two days to catch their first glimpse of the prince. A group of children from Bonington Junior School in Bulwell, Nottingham travelled down to hand a congratulations card to Kensington Palace.

William Arthur Philip Louis

On 4th August, at forty-four days old, William was christened in the Music Room at Buckingham Palace. The Archbishop of Canterbury, Dr Robert Runcie, led the baptism service. The long list of godparents included the former King Constantine of Greece; Lady Susan Hussey, one of the Queen's senior Ladies-in-Waiting; Princess Alexandra; Lord Romsey, Lord Mountbatten's grandson; Sir Laurens van der Post and the Duchess of Westminster.

Opposite: The ceremony took place at 11.00 am and the very hungry baby needed much reassurance from his mother!

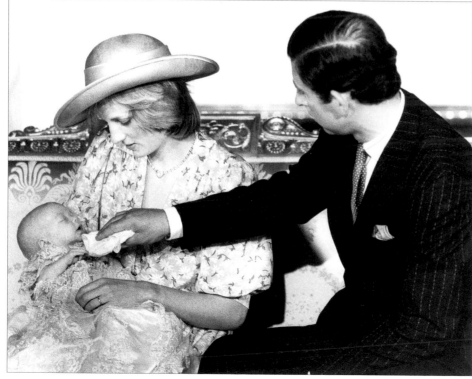

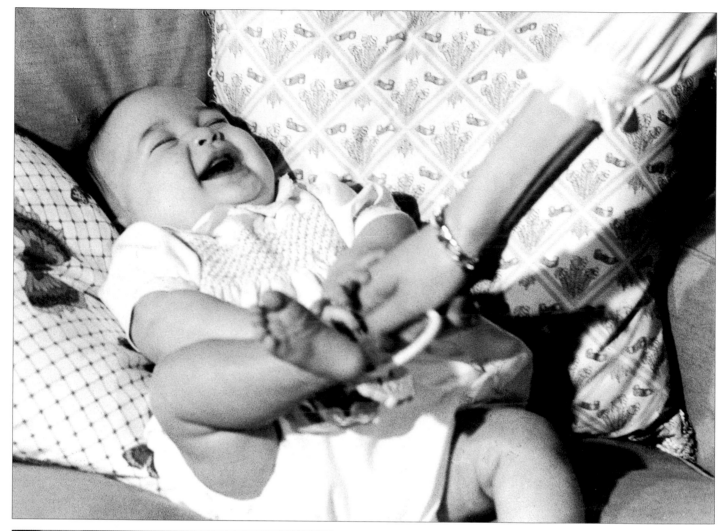

Devoted Parents

Above: William made an official appearance to the cameras just before Christmas in the Princess of Wales's study at Kensington Palace. He was six months old and produced peals of laughter after being tickled by his mother.

Left and opposite: The walled gardens of Kensington Palace provided an ideal playground for the young prince. His parents had always been determined that he would lead as happy and normal a life as possible.

Barbara Barnes had been recruited as his nanny and Olga Powell, a very experienced nursery maid, assisted her. However, both Charles and Diana ensured that they regularly spent time with their son, often taking over feeding and bath times. When Charles and Diana embarked on an official tour of Australia in 1983, both nanny and baby came too so he did not have to endure the long separation from his parents that Charles had experienced as a boy.

Wombat William

As a toddler, William spoke early and had a natural curiosity about the world. During a summer holiday to Balmoral in 1983 he found and pushed a button on the nursery wall, which sent an alarm signal to Aberdeen police station. It was only after the entire estate had been sealed off that it was discovered he was responsible! Another favourite escapade was flushing objects down the toilet, which on one occasion included his father's shoes! It was after a string of mischievous episodes that he earned the nickname of Wombat.

Below: William just before his second birthday in the gardens at Kensington Palace.

Opposite: At the age of two and after a slight pause at the top, he successfully achieved one of the requirements of royal life – descending the very steep steps of an Andover plane of the Queen's Flight!

Expecting a Brother

In September 1984 William flew with Prince Charles to be reunited with his mother in London after a summer holiday in Balmoral. Charles and Diana were expecting their second child at the end of the month and Diana had gone back to London early to see her obstetrician. She eventually gave birth to their second son on 15th September. He was called Henry Charles Albert David but was to be known as Harry. Diana was concerned about sibling jealousy and ensured that William visited his baby brother soon after the birth but it was quickly evident that William was enthralled with his younger brother.

Harry was christened at St George's Chapel in the grounds of Windsor Castle. By now William was often called Wills, an endearment begun by his mother. During the gathering, Wills ran unchecked through the assembled family acting as a constant source of entertainment for them and the press photographers alike!

Miss Mynors' Kindergarten

At the age of three it was time for William to make the transition into childhood. His parents agreed that he needed a more disciplined environment. Although Charles was keen for him to follow tradition and be educated at home, Diana wanted him to mix with other children and make his own friends. After much research and many visits, it was agreed that he would go to Miss Mynors' Kindergarten in Notting Hill Gate. After much preparation including the installation of additional security William arrived for his first day at school in September 1985, gripping a Postman Pat flask.

Right: After his first morning he skipped out proudly waving the paper mouse he had made.

Opposite: In the summer of 1985, William and Harry joined their parents as they boarded the Royal Yacht *Britannia*. It was the start of the Western Isles tour.

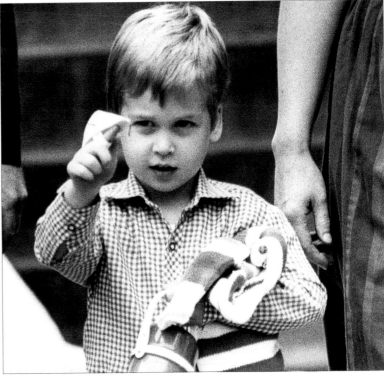

William's First Nativity

Above right and right: At the age of four he had his first opportunity to watch his father play polo. Accompanied by Major Ronald Ferguson and Diana he watched the action at Smith's Lawn, Windsor but had to leave before the end, as it was bath time!

Opposite: William quickly became involved in school activities, taking the role of innkeeper in the Christmas production. It was a very happy school with three classes, each with twelve children. He began in the Cygnets before moving on to Little Swans, then Big Swans. As well as learning in the pre-school environment he had his first opportunity to mix with other children. He soon learned how to pull rank and often his bodyguard would have to intervene to avoid any trouble, but quickly the young prince earned the nickname of 'Basher'.

'Nanny Roof'

Above: William accompanies a playmate to the school nativity.

Opposite: In January 1987, William started at Wetherby, his pre-prep school in Notting Hill, meeting the Headmistress Miss Fredrika Blair Turner. This coincided with the resignation of his nanny Barbara Barnes. Ruth Wallace, whom the boys soon called 'Nanny Roof', replaced her. She was a very businesslike lady who had previously worked for the family of ex-King Constantine of Greece. She was quite a strong disciplinarian and had been given permission by Diana to smack the boys if she felt the occasion warranted such a punishment.

Wetherby School

Left: William happily skipped into school to begin his first day. At the end of the session he proudly showed his artwork to the waiting press *(below left)*.

Again William settled happily into the school environment and soon began to excel at sport. His most notable achievements were in running and the high jump and at Highgrove he was proving to be a very able horseman. He continued to watch his father playing polo *(below right)* and would eventually play himself.

Opposite: William accompanied his parents as Prince Harry started his first day at Chepstow Villas School in Notting Hill Gate.

Sandringham

William also showed a love of traditional country sports and thrived at Sandringham. He watched his first game shoot at the age of four and on each occasion was taught a new skill. By the age of ten he had mastered the basics of how to be a good shot.

Above: On one visit with Peter and Zara Phillips he spotted a 1936 fire engine and delightedly climbed aboard complete with silver helmet.

Opposite: William shakes hands with the Dean of St George's Chapel, Windsor.

The Pre-prep Years

By 1987 Charles had moved out of Kensington Palace and was spending most of his time at Highgrove so William only saw his father at weekends when he would travel to Gloucestershire with Harry and his mother. It was at this time that Diana started taking the boys out for daytrips. These included Alton Towers, go-kart racing, sports fixtures and the theatre. One half-term treat with four friends was a visit to Richmond Theatre to see *Stig of the Dump (left)*.

Opposite above: At Wetherby School Sports Day William enthusiastically took part and came third in the egg and spoon race. Diana entered and won the mothers' race and came away the proud winner of a potted plant!

Opposite left and right: In September 1988, he returned to Wetherby School at the end of the summer break. He eventually emerged at the end of the session proudly wearing a mask he had made that morning.

Above right: On Christmas Day he accompanied his cousin Zara Phillips after the traditional morning service at Sandringham.

Above left: At the age of six he was pageboy at the wedding of Rupert Soames and Camilla Dunne at Hereford Cathedral.

First Outing in Long Trousers!

Although initially hesitant, William enjoyed football and was becoming a skilled player. He would play every week at the school sports grounds in Richmond. He was growing fast and during the Royal Family's Easter break at Windsor he was allowed to wear long trousers for the first time *(opposite)*. The occasion was the Easter Sunday service at St George's Chapel, Windsor.

William was still full of fun and loved to mess around with water pistols on the Highgrove Estate. On one memorable occasion he and Harry were aiming randomly at visitors and made a direct hit on the Queen before they realised it was her. They were often encouraged by Prince Andrew who would also bring his own whoopee cushions along.

Easter Parade

Above: Diana holds the hand of her six-year-old son as they leave St George's Chapel, Windsor Castle, followed by Prince Charles and Zara Phillips after they had attended the traditional Easter Day service.

William continued to enjoy horse riding and took part in a tournament at Minchinhampton in Gloucestershire when he was nearly seven. Most of his experience was on the Highgrove Estate.

Right: Deep in thought at Minchinhampton; the press likened his expression to his father's.

Opposite: Riding lessons at Highgrove with estate groom Maureen Cox.

Mixed Fortunes at Sports Day

William continued to enjoy the times spent on holiday and on the family estates. In May 1989 he was able to spend time on his BMX bike *(left)* while on holiday in the Scilly Isles and in September he was at the Althorp Estate *(below)* for the wedding of the Viscount.

Opposite: There were mixed fortunes at the School Sports Day that summer. William won his heat of the 'goldrush' race and eventually came second in the final. Diana was expected to retain her title in the mothers' race but was also pipped into second place as she sprinted barefoot down the track. Prince Charles unfortunately finished second to last in the father's race.

Final Year at Wetherby

As William began his final year at Wetherby, one of the first events was the annual Harvest Festival at St Matthew's, Bayswater. With a friend he joined the crocodile of children escorted along the road to attend the service. The two indulged in a happy session of horseplay as they made their way from school to the church. William's contribution, leeks, potatoes and carrots, was from his father's first crop of organic vegetables grown in the kitchen gardens at Highgrove. A beaming Princess of Wales joined the other parents to watch from the pews as the children arrived at the church.

Below: On the balcony at Buckingham Palace. To William's left are Lady Rose and Lady Davina Windsor.

Soccer Star

All the practice sessions paid off when William was selected to play for Wetherby School when they took on Bassett House of Kensington in their first football fixture of the season. Despite a shoulder injury, on the pitch he showed great determination and team spirit. He helped his team take a 2-1 lead at half-time at which point he was substituted to enable another child to play.

Steve Baric, the Bassett House sports master, commented that William 'did very well and was not afraid to get stuck in. He seems a very nice lad and if he carries on he could develop into a good prospect. He enjoyed himself, and it's nice he has the chance to play football because it's not a sport normally associated with the Royal Family.'

Working and Playing

Left: William arrived with Harry and his mother to watch the International Showjumping Championships at Olympia.

Right: Charles again took on the challenge of the fathers' race at the annual Sports Day!

Below left: While watching a polo match at Cirencester in 1990, William took the opportunity to mess around with a polo stick at the side of the field!

Below right: Whenever possible, Diana would arrange her schedule to fit around the boys' school timetable.

The Move to Prep School

William's last Sports Day at Wetherby ended in tears after he disobeyed his mother. He ran away when she wanted to go home which resulted in a sharp smack on the backside.

The time had come to select a boarding school for him. Both Charles and Diana had attended boarding schools and agreed that it would help him settle down and understand his responsibilities. Again, much research was done and several visits made. Finally they settled on Ludgrove Preparatory School in Berkshire. It was reasonably close to Highgrove and Kensington Palace and had a friendly atmosphere and a good sporting reputation. Most significantly it was set in 130 acres and was positioned well back from the road, which would give William maximum privacy.

Opposite: In September 1990, Headmaster Gerald Barber met William – his prep school days had begun.

Accident at Ludgrove

Above: After their visit to the Horse of the Year Show William and Harry were taken to the stables where a female Santa invited them on to the sleigh to receive presents.

Left: William deep in study – he is left-handed.

Opposite: Skiing in Austria.

By this time his parents' marriage was all but over with Charles and Diana frequently travelling to functions separately.

In June 1991, William was accidentally hit with a golf club by a friend, which knocked him unconscious with blood pouring from the wound. He was rushed to the Royal Berkshire Hospital for treatment. His parents disagreed over which hospital should treat him but in the end Diana had her wish and he was sent to Great Ormond Street Hospital for Sick Children under police escort. He had a depressed fracture of the skull and needed a seventy-five minute operation to assess the damage that had been caused. Diana stayed with him while Charles had to continue with his royal duties.

William's Close Relationship with Diana

William continued to have a very close relationship with his mother and she called him 'the man in my life'. They were constantly photographed together at official and unofficial functions. On occasions when he had witnessed one of his parents' frequent arguments he would try to comfort her. On one famous occasion he booked a table at her favourite restaurant, San Lorenzo's, in Beauchamp Place, to cheer her up.

Above and left: Wimbledon Women's Final 1991.

Opposite: Soon after his accident he had the opportunity to watch the final practice for the British Grand Prix. Jackie Stewart, racing driver and friend of the Royal Family, hosted the day and William was flown to Silverstone by helicopter. High jinks with Jackie's son Mark showed that he had made a full recovery. He later had the opportunity to jump into the cockpit of the 200mph Benetton Ford that Nelson Piquet had driven.

Back on Top Form

Right: William with former world motor racing champion Jackie Stewart and his son Mark at Silverstone. In jeans, trainers, a promotional sweatshirt and a peaked cap, William showed he was fully recovered from the head injury that led to a stay in hospital.

Below left: Christmas Day at Sandringham, 1991.

Below right: William travelled out with Diana and Harry for a fortnight's skiing holiday in March 1992. Charles joined them for part of the time.

However, the following month Diana's father, Earl Spencer, died from a heart attack and both boys attended the funeral in Northamptonshire. The occasion helped to heal a rift between his children and their stepmother Raine, whom he had married after parting from their mother Frances.

Opposite: William and Harry leaving the dinosaur exhibition at London's Natural History Museum.

Action-packed Days Out

Above and right: During the March skiing trip, William had plenty of opportunity to hone his technique under the tutelage of instructor Markus Kleissel. He was hesitant at first but gradually gained confidence.

Opposite above: During the Easter break, Diana took the boys to Thorpe Park in Surrey. Although personal detectives were with them, they kept a low profile and it proved to be an action-packed day where the boys could behave just like any others - getting soaked on the rides and eating ice cream in between!

Opposite below: In July Jackie Stewart took William to the British Grand Prix at Silverstone where he met Nigel Mansell and was given an autographed tee shirt.

Diana and Charles Separate

Throughout 1992, William's parents' marriage continued to crumble and on 9th December Prime Minister John Major announced in the House of Commons that Charles and Diana would be separating. The day before Diana had driven to Ludgrove to tell William and his incredibly mature response was 'I hope you will both be happier now'.

Right and below left: William was obviously enthralled by all the noise and action at Silverstone and videoed some of the practice sessions. He again had the opportunity to sit at the controls of the Benetton Ford.

Below right: In their October half term, Diana took the boys to Buckmore Park near Rochester in Kent. She had bought the go-karts for them and they confidently raced the machines around the track at speeds up to 50mph.

Opposite: Back on the slopes in Austria in 1993.

Confidence grows

Opposite above left and right: Further skiing holidays as his skill and confidence grow.

Opposite below: William and Harry attended the Easter Service at St George's Chapel with the Queen Mother in 1994.

Left: William arrives at Wimbledon to watch the women's final.

Below left: William leaves the Chicago Rib Shack in Knightsbridge in January 1995.

Below right: William with his father.

At Easter 1993 Tiggy Legge-Bourke entered William's life. She was officially employed as an assistant to Charles's private secretary but in reality she was there to befriend and look after the boys whenever they were staying with Charles. She would challenge him in sport but also act as mentor and confidante and as a result, William quickly grew very close to her.

William Begins his Years at Eton

William had thoroughly enjoyed his last year at Ludgrove and was developing into a charming teenager. His manners were impeccable; he was a fine athlete and had achieved high academic standards. As a result he successfully passed his Common Entrance examination to Eton College.

He had his own study-cum-bedroom and the one extra privilege of a private bathroom. The Matron of the Manor House, Elizabeth Heathcote, looked him after. The Dames at Eton are like surrogate mothers, being responsible for the boys' emotional needs and there to guide them through their school life. He also had his own personal tutor Mr Stuart-Clarke whom he would see for two hours every week. He settled into school life very quickly.

In September 1995 he arrived at the school for his first day. Despite the fact that his parents were in the midst of divorce proceedings the whole family arrived together.

The Eton Years

William spent five very happy years at Eton. The school has a very strong pastoral system and William was able to be anonymous. Inside the school he was away from the eyes of the press and he thrived on the stability and care that he received.

There he achieved both academic and sporting success. He gained nine GCSEs and three 'A' levels. He was a fearless footballer and was soon selected for his year's First XI. He enjoyed rowing and spent much of the summer term in 1997 sculling on the Thames. He then switched to swimming and was one of the country's top 100 swimmers in the 50-metre freestyle for his age group, breaking the Berkshire Schools' record in 1998. With serious training he could possibly have made the national squad but there were major complications over time needed for training and security.

Right and overleaf: William strides out with his classmates on his first day.

William's Confirmation

William was confirmed in March 1997 at St George's Chapel, Windsor. By the age of fourteen he was already six feet tall. It was the first time Charles and Diana had been seen together in public since their divorce the previous August.

Opposite: The family leave after the service.

Above: Walking by the River Dee in Scotland while on holiday with his father in August 1997, just days before his mother's tragic death.

Diana, Princess of Wales

William was on holiday at Balmoral with Harry and his father when Diana was killed in the car crash in Paris on 31st August 1997. She died in the night and the boys were woken by Charles in the morning and told of the accident. That morning they both chose to join the family for the traditional Sunday service at Crathie. Tiggy immediately flew to Scotland and was invaluable in helping them cope with the grief that followed. Overnight William had to grow up very quickly. He helped his father plan her funeral and the bond between them grew ever stronger from that day.

William, Harry, Prince Charles, Earl Spencer and Prince Philip walked behind the cortège as it set off from St James's Palace and made its way to Westminster Abbey. 2,000 people, 500 of whom represented her favourite charities, attended the funeral service. After the funeral a hearse took the coffin to the Althorp Estate in Northamptonshire. She was buried in a private family service on an island in the middle of a lake.

In the weeks that followed the protective atmosphere of Eton and the friends that he had made there, also helped him cope with the loss of his mother.

William on the Road

William had his first driving lesson at Highgrove with police driving instructor Sergeant Chris Gilbert on 26th July 1999, the start of his summer holidays from Eton. He drove a Ford Focus.

During the summer of 1999 he began taking polo lessons with a member of the Guards Polo Club, which is based in Windsor Great Park. This was his father's old club. He was an able rider and picked up the basics of the game quickly. Many hope that his involvement in the game will raise the profile of the sport.

Queen Mother's 99th Birthday

Below: William attended the celebrations for the Queen Mother's 99th birthday and joined the photo call outside Clarence House.

Opposite and left: A proud William after his driving lesson.

At the end of 1999 Tiggy Legge-Bourke married and left royal employment. Ruth Clarke joined the staff to take care of William's and Harry's affairs but obviously has a very different relationship to the boys. Her role is very much office-based, looking after diaries and responding to all correspondence.

William's Anger at Publication

Charles stood by William's side at the Highgrove Estate as William spoke of his and Harry's anger over the publication of the book by Princess Diana's former private secretary, Patrick Jephson, about the Princess of Wales. Speaking very calmly he said, 'Of course Harry and I are both quite upset about it - that our mother's trust has been betrayed'. He had met the press to discuss the plans for his gap year prior to studying History of Art at St Andrews University when he voiced his condemnation of the book.

Gap Year in Chile

Through the Raleigh International organisation William spent three months in Chile in the foothills of the Patagonian Mountains. Part of the time was spent working with 100 other young people and 40 volunteers and he 'mucked in' with the most menial or difficult tasks. The group were responsible for building projects in the village and he worked alongside the others. He loved the fact that he had improved the villagers' lives.

Opposite: William visited the Tabernacle in Cardiff after attending the television programme *Songs of Praise* recorded at the Millennium Stadium.

Skiing with Dad

There was still time for family holidays and William and Harry joined their father at Klosters, Switzerland. It was soon noticed that both princes now towered over their father!

During his gap year he also spent time in southern Africa. In Botswana he took part in culling some animals and lived rough while tracking others. He was granted a licence from the government to shoot wild game. Most nights were spent under canvas.

He also went to Belize with the Welsh Guards on jungle training exercise and worked on a dairy farm in south-west England as a farm labourer. He reportedly thrived on the simple life he led, getting up at 4.30am and just being another helper on the farm with no special privileges and total anonymity.

Family Celebrations

William joined the family for the thanksgiving service at St Paul's Cathedral, to celebrate the Queen Mother's life, just ahead of her 100th birthday.

Below: William with his cousin Peter Phillips after the service. They have always been great friends and Peter, who is four years older, has always been very protective of William.

Opposite top and below left: William visited the Anchor Mills Project in Paisley, Scotland.

Opposite below right: William attends the 10th anniversary party of the Press Complaints Commission held at Somerset House, London.

St Andrews University

After his gap year, William took up a place at St Andrews University in Scotland to read History of Art. He had always wanted to study in Scotland and was reportedly attracted to the university on the Fife coast first, and the course second. He had achieved a B in his Art 'A' level, A in Geography and C in Biology. He lived in a Hall of Residence and opted not to travel up for the Freshers' Week because he was worried about the media attention that it might attract. His father drove him up for the start of the second week.

Below left: Prince William attended the St Andrews University Fashion Show. The show was sponsored by the French designer Yves St Laurent and was expected to raise £5,000 for charity. Students had paid £15 for a ticket and £200 for a VIP table.

Opposite: Prince William holding flowers as members of the Royal Family gather for the traditional Christmas Day service at Saint Mary Magdalen church, Sandringham.

Death of the Queen Mother

His great-grandmother, the Queen Mother, died on 30th March 2002. She was 101 and there had been concern for her health for many months. William followed the gun carriage that carried her coffin from the Queen's Chapel, St James's Palace. The ceremonial procession made its way to Westminster Hall and thousands of mourners lined the route to pay their last respects before filing past her coffin as she lay in state.

Her funeral was held four days later on 9th April and she was then interred at St George's Chapel, Windsor, next to her late husband King George VI.

Opposite: William walks down The Mall with Harry in the ceremonial procession to the lying-in-state.

Above: Left to right: Viscount Linley, Prince William, Prince Harry, Peter Phillips.

Left: The emotion and strain show on the faces of the two brothers.

The Golden Jubilee

Above: William arrives to join the congregation of the Golden Jubilee Service of Thanksgiving at St Paul's Cathedral in London on 4th June 2002.

Opposite top: William and Harry watch the flypast from the balcony at Buckingham Palace. The twenty-seven aircraft including the Red Arrows and Concorde flew over The Mall as part of the final celebrations. It was the largest formation flight over London since 1981.

Opposite bottom: Prince William, Prince Charles and The Queen all sharing in the fun.

Celebrations at St Paul's Cathedral

Left and opposite: Prince William and his uncle Prince Andrew travel together in an open carriage.

Below: Members of the Royal Family gather together on the steps at St Paul's Cathedral.

The Queen and Prince Philip travelled in the Gold State Coach and were escorted by Princess Anne and the Prince of Wales on horseback. The coach was built for King George III in 1762 and has only been used by the Queen twice before - her Coronation and the Silver Jubilee. She then had lunch at the Guildhall before watching the parade and carnival along The Mall.

William goes walkabout

The celebratory parade lasted more than three hours and included bands from the Notting Hill Carnival, voluntary service personnel, children from the Chicken Shed Theatre Company and a series of living rooms reflecting the five decades of the Queen's reign. When it finished, the Royal Family went on to the balcony at Buckingham Palace to watch the flypast.

Right: Prince Charles, Prince Harry and Prince William inside St.Paul's Cathedral.

Below left: The princes watch the parade with their father.

Below right and opposite top: William on walkabout along The Mall.

Opposite below: William with Claudia Schiffer at Ashe Park in Hampshire, June 2002. She had just presented him with the Porcelanosa Cup as a member of the winning polo team during a charity competition.

ACKNOWLEDGEMENTS

The photographs in this book are from the archives of the *Daily Mail*.
Particular thanks to Steve Torrington, Dave Sheppard, Brian Jackson, Alan Pinnock,
Richard Jones and all the staff.

Thanks also to Cliff Salter, Richard Betts,
Peter Wright, Trevor Bunting and Simon Taylor.
Design by John Dunne.